More Than A Message

More Than A Message

Southside Dragons

AuthorHouse™
1663 Liberty Drive
Bloomington, IN 47403
www.authorhouse.com
Phone: 1-800-839-8640

© 2011 Southside Dragons. All rights reserved.

No part of this book may be reproduced, stored in a retrieval system, or transmitted by any means without the written permission of the author.

First published by AuthorHouse   10/19/2011

ISBN: 978-1-4634-2998-0 (sc)
ISBN: 978-1-4634-2997-3 (hc)
ISBN: 978-1-4634-2996-6 (ebk)

Library of Congress Control Number: 2011911530

Printed in the United States of America

Any people depicted in stock imagery provided by Thinkstock are models, and such images are being used for illustrative purposes only. Certain stock imagery © Thinkstock.

This book is printed on acid-free paper.

Because of the dynamic nature of the Internet, any web addresses or links contained in this book may have changed since publication and may no longer be valid. The views expressed in this work are solely those of the author and do not necessarily reflect the views of the publisher, and the publisher hereby disclaims any responsibility for them.

About the Authors:

Matt Molner

I am from Queen of All Saints parish in St. Louis, Missouri. I also went to grade school and played sports there. I currently am an honors student and play soccer and baseball. In the future I see myself as an architect or engineer of some sort, with a small family of my own. I feel this book could be a huge success because it has great potential and each student has put a great deal of time and effort into it.

Anthony Cataldo

I am sixteen years old and I am from St. Louis, Missouri. I am from St Gabriel the Archangel Parish where I attended grade school. I currently attend St. Mary's High School, where I am President of my class, an all Honors student, and a Soccer State Champion. In twenty years, I see myself as a very successful dentist living in my hometown with a happy family. I feel that this book is filled with inspiring words from some of the brightest young men I have ever had the privilege of meeting. This book will shock the reader opening up a part of the mind and soul that some do not realize exists. It is a work of art and I am very proud to be a part of it.

Conor Cashner

I was born September sixth 1994 in Barnes-Jewish Hospital in St. Louis Missouri. I currently attend Saint Mary's High School and am an honors student. I am interested in a career in teaching.

Jack Ruzicka

I am from Immaculate Heart of Mary Parish (I.H.M.), and I attended I.H.M. grade school. I am presently a sophomore at St. Mary's High School. At St.Mary's, I participate in the theater as an actor. I am also a student ambassador, High School Night speaker, and I am the Spirit Representative in the St. Mary's Student Council. My interests include acting, playing drums, making people laugh, and drinking Pepsi.

I am not quite sure where I see myself in twenty years. I kind of see myself as a priest, but I can also see myself married and being involved in youth ministry. I know I will be serving the Lord.

I think this book is just a small and peaceful way for people to realize that there are people in this world who truly love Christ, especially the teenagers in our society. If I were asked the question: What do you hate most about being a teenager? I would answer: That all, or most, teenagers are stereotyped into being nothing but obnoxious troublemakers who don't give a care about anyone else in the world but themselves. Yes, there are teenagers who don't make the best decisions, but there are kids out there who love, and care for other people and other things. I believe that this book proves that.

Brandon Polito

I am from Epiphany of Our Lord parish in St. Louis, Missouri. I enjoy hanging out with my friends and playing sports. I play football; I also wrestle and throw track and field for my high school.
What I think about this book? I think this book was a great experience for me to have. It was a lot of fun to do it too.
Where will I be 20 years from now? I have no clue at this moment, I hope to have a good job and a good family in 20 years but I am not exactly sure where or how I'm going to get there yet.

Nicholas Ryan

I attended Queen of All Saints from kindergarten to 8th grade. I attend mass at Queen of All Saints every weekend. In my spare time, I like to play sports, video games, and hang out with friends. My favorite sport is hockey. In twenty years, I see myself in the field of accounting or internet technology. I think the book is a great way for me to connect with myself in poetry.

Jimmy Christian Leo Tietjens

My parish is St. Margaret Mary Alacoque, which I attended from kindergarten through 5th grade. I then left and went to public schooling till high school. My hobbies and interests are playing airsoft, soccer, X-BOX 360, and I love hanging out with friends and having fun, I also invest in silver bullion when I have some extra money.
(The Cover Image is an original work by Jimmy)

Stephen Allen Stephen Trae Showers III

For grade school I attended two schools. For K-4th grade I went to Resurrection of our Lord, and for 5-8 I went to Immaculate Heart of Mary. I guess I'm an athletic person. I play soccer in the fall and volleyball in spring. On most nights, though, I can be found on Xbox Live, playing one game or another. I like to write short stories and just brainstorming about ideas. I'm also a big computer nerd. I've been teaching myself to program for the past few years and I've been told that I'm good at it. I may pursue it as a job if not a career in the future. In twenty years, honestly, I see myself married with maybe two children, living in the county, probably not the wealthiest family but not poor either, at a point where we can afford some nice things but not everything. I think the book is really something that a lot of people should do. I have always enjoyed writing, but I've never really put words down on paper that came from me, the actual me.

Devin Belvin

I went to Epiphany of Our Lord for grades 1-8, and then chose to attend St. Mary's High School. I enjoy playing all sports, whether organized or not, especially with my friends. In 20 years, I see myself with a steady job, maybe having to do with law, and a growing family. I think that our book is a very creative idea that will turn out well.

Luke Alexander Wolfgang Guy

I went to Immaculate Heart of Mary grade school for kindergarten-8th grade. I play soccer and volleyball and like to play video games and hang out with my friends.

I see myself in my own house with my wife. I hope to be working somewhere with animals or doing something with math like teaching or accounting.

I think that this book will be very good because we have a couple really good poets in our class who really like to sit down and write their poems. We also have students in our class who are trying really hard to put this book together and find ways and places to sell the books.

James Muehlenkamp

When I was in grade school, if someone had told me I would be the co-author of a published poetry book I would have said they were crazy. Looking back on what I was, I realize now that St. Mary's has really taught me to be more open about new things. I've changed so much that I feel like a new person. Even though this book isn't my idea, I am glad to be part of it. Hunting has been a passion of mine for a long time and now Theater is too. I am an all honors student with a high GPA. I play X-Box in my free time. My LIVE gamertag is JTC Muehlenkamp. I am happy that I am who I am.

John Specker

I went to Seven Holy Founders for grade school. I am interested in all sports, and I enjoy playing them. I play baseball, basketball, and football. I do not know where I see myself in twenty years, but I would like to follow a career as a firefighter or a policeman.

I had an enjoyable time working on this book, because we could understand others' ways of thinking.

Kevin Hennessy

I am from St.Stephen Protomartyr parish. I play baseball, basketball, and football for my high school. I enjoy hanging out with my friends.

Where do I see myself in twenty years, seriously? Hmmm? In twenty years I think I will have a wife and kids. Hopefully I will be a successful sports agent.

What do I think about this book?

I had a good time writing this book and we all got to compare our poems to some of the great poets. It was a good experience for all of us.

Brendan Joseph DuVall

I was named after two pro hockey players Brendan Shannahan, and Curtis Joseph.
My parish is currently St. Gabriel's church. I went to multiple schools. I went to St. Mary Magdalene and three different schools in Affton. Then I went to St. Gabriel for three years. My current interests are hockey, football and volleyball. In twenty years I see myself being a physical therapist. I would be working with sporting injuries such as a torn acl or mcl.
I think the book is really fun to do; it gets the class together to do something big. I did not think making a book would be this fun.

Acknowledgements

We, the Southside Dragons, would like to give special thanks to:
Fr. Mitch Doyen—He inspired our creativity
Zip Rzeppa and Rob Vogel—They let us donate our proceeds to the Society of St. Vincent de Paul
Archbishop Robert Carlson—He wrote the Foreword to our poetry book
Our Parents—For supporting us throughout our lives in everything we do
Clarence Heller, '74,—He showed us how to express ourselves through poetry
Faculty and Staff—They helped give feedback on our poems
Ms. Griffin's Graphic Arts Class—Who helped design our book and prepare it for submission to the publisher.

FOREWORD

<u>More Than a Message</u> is a significant contribution to the work of the New Evangelization. I have consistently pledged my support for the great ministry of Catholic Education because I firmly believe that our young people are not only our future; they are proclaiming the Gospel with their lives today. We have much to learn from our young people. Their openness to God's Spirit, their desire to know Jesus more deeply and their commitment to follow Him are all signs to us that our Church and our world are in very capable hands, the hands of God and the hands of our young people. Whether visiting a parish and meeting with students in one of our elementary schools or having the privilege of confirming young disciples who are beginning their teenage years, I am continually impressed by the capacity of our young people to bring us to Christ. That is the importance of the New Evangelization, the deepening of our relationship with Jesus so that we can witness His love to the world.

These young men from St. Mary's High School have provided this great gift to the Church. Their poems allow us to glimpse their lives. From the sacred to the profane, from the profound to the ridiculous, these poems prompt us to laugh, perhaps to cry sometimes and certainly to pray at all times.

Trae invites us to see a communion, which is God's deepest desire for us. Jack seeks a peace which must yet be possible in our day. Anthony turns a bout with the flu into a reflection of the soul. Jimmy invites us to remember, or discover for the first time, the difficult struggle of being true to ourselves. Brandon protests the writing of a poem and creates a good one along the way. James allows his own grief to inspire a plea for hope. Brendan wants to be faithful, but he is very much aware of the struggle to become a good man. John started slow, but being stuck frees his soul to express more poetry. Conor uses his intellect to teach us about the Eucharist. Kevin invites us to let Jesus all the way into our lives. Nick encourages us to make the most with what we have been given. Devin offers a peek at what it is really like to be fifteen. Luke challenges us with some very practical advice. And Matt makes us smile and think at the same time.

This little book of poems is yet unfinished. We can almost see the hearts of these young authors expanding. There are hints of hope, but nothing is certain. It is more than a message, because it is an invitation for all of us to carry on the most important work of the new evangelization. We can certainly rededicate ourselves to the mission of Catholic Education in our great Archdiocese of St. Louis.

I am grateful to these young men for sharing this work with us. I am grateful, too, for their collaboration with the St. Louis Society of St. Vincent de Paul. All proceeds from the sale of this book will benefit the charitable mission of the Society. It is for us, then, a double blessing.

Most Reverend Robert J. Carlson
Archbishop of St. Louis
May 1, 2011

More than a Message

"Hear, O Israel! The Lord is our God, the Lord alone! Therefore, you shall love the Lord, your God, with all your heart, and with all your soul, and with all your strength."
Dt 6:4-5

Southside Dragons

Act I - Mind

"Now you, brothers, like Isaac, are children of the promise. But just as then the child of the flesh persecuted the child of the spirit, it is the same now."

Gal 4:28-29

God's Emblem

As God should be the Genesis of our lives,
I know that the Genesis of his life is all of us,
within his Genesis is billions of individuals.
In God's point of view we are the prestige edition of his emblem.
All of our emblems are rusty and cracked and could be rubbed enough
where you can't even see your own names of who we are.

Polish your emblem, fix it, upgrade it to a precious metal,
make it shine bright enough where God can see it from the heavens,
the glow of your emblem will set a better tone on yourself
and others' whose are tarnished.

Jimmy Tietjens

Communion

What is this all about?
Bread & Wine
Or Body & Blood
Jesus comes to us through it.

He said eat my body and drink my blood you will live
Live forever in his kingdom.
Is that all you have to do?
Is there something more you need to do?

If so, what is it?
Live like Jesus.
That is what the bible says.
But can anybody do that?
Can you ever be completely perfect?

John Specker

Fulfilling Hope

I never know if the truth or dishonesty lies behind the smile that's worth a thousand words, but that one single word doesn't seem to come to mind.
And with one last anxious breath; I fall back into my thoughts, frozen in time.
My hope is asleep, but desire alive. Please wake me up before I leave here again.
I tried my best to fix the problem and precious time doesn't mean a thing.
Amongst the vastness, through all the blackness one single star shines in the sky.
I try to conquer this loneliness with admiration, an appetite so bold, but how weary the success seems to be. If blinding disaster may come between us, release an everlasting sign to materialize The Dream.

Anthony Cataldo

A Sign

We look at the world, wondering,
Where miracles occur?
We are too narrow minded to realize,
that there is a miracle,
constant, ever present, always in motion.

We eat and drink and are blessed,
the Eucharist is
salvation, liberation, time away
from this world, with the one we love.

Eucharist is bread and wine,
Eucharist is love.

Conor Cashner

Who am I?

Why am I me?
What if I had different parents?
What if I was an animal, would I still be ME?
God makes us in his image, but what does he look like?
It is said that he has a plan for everything,
So there must be a reason that I am who I am.
What is it . . . ?

James Muehlenkamp

What's the Truth?

There are two stories to life
There's the story of God
What's the truth?
We are taught to believe that God made
everything and everyone,
That God is almighty and no one greater than him

We are taught that humans come from evolution
We are taught that there's a scientific fact
about everything that happens; What's the truth?
Could God just be another made up person that has great powers like
superman?
Could The Big Bang Theory be wrong?
and God be the real creator of everything . . .
WHAT'S THE TRUTH?

Brandon Polito

A COMPLICATEDLY SIMPLE IDEA

I will always come, but I am never there.
I hold much for some, little for others.
I bring everything, and I bring nothing.
When I arrive, I change.

You will never know me, even though I am a part of life.
But I am always waiting for you, even thought I can't be reached.
If you do find me, I become something else.
But I am obvious.

I am taken for granted too often.
I am tomorrow.
And I am coming, with or without you . . .

James Muehlenkamp

Southside Dragons

Our Future

God gives us the right,
The right to choose between good and bad,
And the way we make our choices,
Is going to shape our future,

Our future with ourselves, with God,
with friends and family,
So we should hopefully choose
to make our future better with all those people,
And especially with the person that has given us this right, God

Brandon Polito

In Search of Me

So many before me,
So where do I go to find out
They all shaped what shapes me
I would not be here without them

I want to learn from what they said.
But I don't know how to do so
I try I really do
But I only end up confused. I listen to them but do not hear their message.

I look it over but do not feel fulfilled
I go for guidance all they do is turn me away
So I will search
'Til I find out what the word actually means.

John Specker

WHY?

Why are there so many questions?
Why does searching for answers only seem to bring more questions?
When men do evil, when groups debate, when couples argue, Why doesn't God stop it?
How can we follow someone who exists without physical proof?
I believe that God makes it so that having faith is hard.
I believe that God requires devotion,
not empty promises to follow him.
The pathway to hell is paved with good INTENTIONS.
The pathway to heaven is paved with good ACTIONS.

James Muehlenkamp

A Sudden Departure

It is one thing to slowly fade, getting those last few moments, not leaving behind regret, but just feeling like an eternity is too soon. It's another to be seized at any moment. To be gone before a goodbye was even a thought. Within one precious moment lifetimes of dreams and hopes immediately drop into the laps of the vulnerable ones surrounding you. There is no waking up from this terrible nightmare, no taking back time. This is real. This truth lingers for a moment and then leaves bringing back the unnatural feeling of questioning what is really happening. But there is hope. This last chance at regaining control of what is happening can be found in the memories. The faces and sounds of a time not that long ago when our emotions were part of the present. Both good and bad, these memories are the channels that bring us closer. They are the one thing keeping us connected. Though we might not be everlasting, our memories are and though we may have passed, our memories are rooted into our hearts alive and growing.

Anthony Cataldo

Southside Dragons

The Mind's Malady

It is like being at the divide between reality and the never ending world of hallucination.
It grasps and scrapes away at what is left of your sanity.
It slowly drives you mad with its mockery of your own delusion.
Its insufferable presence drowns your hope with agony and relentless pain.
The only way to escape is to fall back into slumber and get away, but only for a short time.
Before too long, I come back and it lays there tenacious and sturdy, not moving an inch, not feeling any sympathy.
I can only hope that it will not be long before I can escape this taunting and vexatious illness.

Anthony Cataldo

"How long will you people mock my honor, love what is worthless, chase after lies?" Ps 4:3

Southside Dragons

The House

Our lives are like a house filled with many different rooms
We open the front door so that many people may come in and stay
But for some of those people we open the back door so they can leave
It is our choice who we let lounge in our house and who we kick out
We should also ask ourselves: who are these people we let stay?
Has Jesus come in fully to our house?
Did we offer him a drink or snack and let him sit on your couch?
Or did we open the back door like we did for so many others . . . .

Kevin Hennessy

"Love the Lord your God therefore and always heed his charge; his statutes, decrees and commandments." Dt. 11:1

TIME

What does our life run on but time.
Do we ever think about how much time has gone by, how much time we still have, and what we are planning to do with our time?
Time is of the essence as we only have one life to live.
Our life flies by in a small matter of time.
We need to live that small matter of time to the fullest.
Do we ever ask ourselves if we are happy with how we have spent our time in our lives?
Do we ever ask ourselves what we have planned for our lives?
We have a small amount of time on earth, so we must use it wisely.
Time is not based upon clocks.
Time is based upon how WE interpret time.
Time is only a word, but stands for something in our lives.
So how do we interpret time?
Are we living happily in our lives? Is our time a happy time?
Time is not just seconds going by, but our life quickly flying by.

Nick Ryan

Act II-Heart

"I have the strength for everything through him who empowers me."
Philippians 4:13

Southside Dragons

With All Strength

Somehow in this life, I know there's a way
To live out that saying I hear people say:
"You only got one life. Live it to the fullest."
But how?

We live in a world that's troubled with hate.
Sometimes it feels as if we are trapped inside a room.
And the only thing in it is a window.
On the other side of the window is the world we live in.

The window gets smudged and stained with our hate, lust, revenge,
grudges, curses, and negativity.
We often find ourselves looking on helplessly and silently.
We no longer recognize the world, OUR world.

And, sometimes, we no longer recognize ourselves.
We wait patiently for God's grace, to rain down and cleanse our world
and our lives.
And with all strength, we gather ourselves and live for His glory.
And battling against temptation's evil pull, We will live our lives to the
full.

Jack Ruzicka

This The Battle

I wake up in the morning
and I wonder who I am.

I do not know why this is happening;
I face a challenge every day.

Why does it have to be this way?

I'm in a cave and it's collapsing.
There's a bull in my way
And I have to face it.

I fight my way through.
I win the battle
But I lose the war.

Brendan Duvall

Speak Now

Many people wonder and question themselves:
"Who am I?"
"Why am I here?"
You only have one life to live, one life to be yourself,
One life to be the best you can be.
You may be able to stop a clock,
But you cannot stop time
Make yourself known, make yourself heard,
Listen to your heart, and let everyone know what it says.

Matt Molner

Southside Dragons

Alone

I'm alone out here
I don't know how I came to be
All they do is judge
Because they don't understand me
Show me what to do
So that I may fit in alright
But until that day is here
I'm afraid I must keep out of sight.

Devin Belvin

"You are the man!" 2Sam 12:7

|*Life*|

It's funny how life can go
We all fall down the same way
Staring death right in the face
Please pull me up out of this place

I never thought I'd have to come here, stay here, no
I didn't know
I didn't think I'd have to give so much and receive so little
What am I left with
What can I lose
Or will I even get to choose
Will I reach the point of no return
I step into the fire but I only get burned

It's funny how life can go
We all fall down the same way
Staring death right in the face
Please pull me up out of this place

I feel like all eyes are on me
Like I'm supposed to bring forth a change
Doing it all solo
I can't handle this
But I know this knowledge can save lives
Keep families closely tied
Two kids and working parents
A whole family

More Than A Message

Not broken up like most these days
Smart decisions are so abnormal
But we can peek through the keyhole
Spy on a better life
It's on the other side of the door
We just have to push a tad bit more

It's funny how life can go
We all fall down the same way
Staring death right in the face
Please pull me up out of this place

Trae Showers

Acceptance

Do we know what is important in our life?
Do we think we do?
Sports, family, friends and games
Those are all great treasures that we have

But none of those can give us true life
Like Jesus is able to with the Eucharist that he offers to us
Do we accept Jesus like few are able to do?
Or do we turn away from him, and not trust in him because it is easier
that way

Kevin Hennessy

The Ever-lasting Emotion

Every time I think, someone is always on my mind.
Most of the time it is family, friends or faith.
I don't think a day has passed when I didn't think of someone I love.
Love is a word that is tossed around far too often.
Yet, I think that it applies.

Love is what I feel.

By James Muehlenkamp

"We, indeed, are suffering because of our sins."
2Maccabees 7:32

The Lonely Broken Road

I must watch my step
the ice I walk is paper-thin

One wrong move leaves me
helpless as it's caving in

Broken as it is
why'd I choose to come out here

Driven by danger
ignorant of all my fears

Down the path I see
another person far along

Walking aimlessly
no goal in sight, yet his will so strong

The closer I become
to this man of mystery

I finally see now
He's lost, alone, and just like me

I still will follow him
For that's the only thing I know

Walking my whole life through
No love, no joy, just sadness and cold.

Devin Belvin

"The Lord then said to Joshua, 'Do not be afraid or dismayed.'"
Joshua 8:1

Generations

Parent of a Child
You should treat a child how you wanted to be treated
Show the children the good in life
Show them Jesus
Show them love
If you show them love
They might grow up
To help save this sphere of waste
That we call earth
If you show them love
They will help you when you get old
If you show them love
They will show you love too

Luke Guy

Southside Dragons

Be Yourself

Why do we always write in between the lines?
What's wrong with writing on them?
It's okay to be different,
It might be better than being normal
because normal can become boring
I guess what I'm trying to say is . . .
BE YOURSELF!

Matt Molner

Mary and Mom

God has given a mother to me, it is a gift I can never repay.
We are made in God's image, it is the truth, the gift of his love is the proof, And that is why you can always believe, because God will never leave.
So look it up in the Bible, God is always reliable.
Believe this and you will know, God will be wherever you go.

James Muehlenkamp

An Ode to Grief

"... Who will tell of his posterity? For his life is taken from the earth."
Acts 8:33

This poem was written shortly after the loss of a great friend and I would like to dedicate this poem to the late Dan Maddock

What is life but dying?
It always ends in death.
Our bodies are not designed to last,
but why are we left to suffer?

It is so quick that one may think it peaceful.
But any soul who passes on leaves their beloved broken and dead of spirit.
Why would anyone create such a cycle of pain and death?

Life always ends, memories always last,
Until their carriers leave this world and then the memories fade.

But why do objects last?
Any priceless relic should be valued not for its age but for who held it first.
Is life the work of a savior or a madman?
What is the point of free will if God has a plan for everyone?
And why does it always end in death?

If only we could shut it out, reject the Lord.
But doing so will drown one in a pool of ignorance.
If you pray that there is a Heaven for you, a Heaven you will find.

Existence is a cruel punishment, but those who accept this will live on.
But for now, they suffer.

James Muehlenkamp

Act III-Soul

Southside Dragons

The World Weeps

A sadness is wrought from spent shells
that litter the battle scorched earth.
Proclamations are sung of victory and dominance,
yet no one has or can win.
After thousands of years we
Have yet to realize this;
an angel's tear has fallen upon us,
but we shouldered it away in denial.
We are walking down the path of exile,
unaware of our surroundings.
But a road mistaken can be corrected when
given a second chance.
Let us pray that we do not misuse it once more;
there's almost nothing left to lose.

Trae Showers

"They shall beat their swords into plow shares and their spears into pruning hooks" Isaiah 2:4

Untitled

A soldier sets his rifle down, and removes his helmet.
He wipes the perspiration from his forehead and sighs.
This soldier is a sergeant, and he is in charge of a squad.
He looks up at the sky, and sighs.

Another man was killed under his command today.
First, he thinks of his wife back home.
He thinks not only of his wife, but also of his young boy, who is 7 years old now.
He thinks of the way his son giggles with delight as he plays with his toys in the dirt outside.
He thinks of the way his son's hair feels against his lips when he kisses him on the head.
He thinks of his son's smile, and how it brings him to tears.

Then, he thinks of the dead man's family.
He thinks of how that man will never be able to return home, and hold his wife dearly in his arms.
He thinks of how that man will never be able to watch his son grow.
He'll never teach him how to drive, never see him move on to high school, never see him graduate, and never be able to say, "I love you my son. I am proud of you."
The sergeant weeps.

No matter the situation, there is hope.
There may not be a whole lot you can do about it,
But what you can do is pick yourself up,
And keep on marching.
No matter how hard you fall, you can get up stronger.
And God, our Father, looks down from the Heavens and says,
"I love you, my son.
I am proud of you."

Jack Ruzicka

Two Sides

Patience more or less a virtue and easy to the soul.

Alive and filled with passion and everlasting potential. Awakening the spirits of many and enjoying every second of it. Progressing towards a bright future, while still making something of what is left of the present. Creating opportunities and opening doors to incredible places never thought imaginable. Tearing down walls of confusion and doubt. Working hard and never forgetting to be honest. Learning everyday and teaching some as well. A sign of self confidence and and never giving up. Never forgetting to be *real*.

Not here or there. Lost in a thick cloud of blackness too miserable to create even a memory. Gradually filling with self pity and agony. Too blind to realize the truth. Anger growing rapid and doubt drowning my thoughts. Quickly shedding the bright, radiant skin that makes a person who they are. Becoming different and false. Trying to gain, yet losing more in the process. Losing touch with reality, and worse, the joys of life and love. Completely False and misguided.

Anthony Cataldo

Afterlife

Is there such thing as afterlife?
You live for so long,
And you are finished with this world.
You are put in the ground.

The story is that based on how you lived your life
You lived it to the fullest and did right by God you will become one with him in heaven.
If you lived it to the fullest but not the way God would want you to you go to HELL.

So your body is in the ground with the worms.
But you soul apparently moves on.
It goes somewhere.
Or does it?
Is there really a place where everybody lives in harmony?
Is there a place where everyone lives in heat and fire?
I guess there is but how is it proven.
While still living you have no true answer.

So you have to pray. There is something you can do
And that is live how the bible says.
You have no proof that anything good will come from doing so.
So you have to have this word called Faith.

But is faith really enough?
Do you have the faith that there is something after this?
Other than just a hole that is filled with a concrete container,
Which holds you there forever?
Does your soul really move on to this Afterlife?

John Specker

His Message; Our Avenue

Born to life, with much to see. Embracing the time with every possibility.
Now life has been withdrawn, another fateful sigh.
Silence is broken with another lonely cry.
So soft it seems, but deep it goes.

Through these abandoned streets, it seems to freely roam.
Anticipation is only a dream, and optimism was left behind.
Becoming familiar with the worst of extremes, if you find yourself lost just look to the sky.
And when you're at your last breathe, and seem to be falling. Just speak my name so I know that you're calling.

You're not at the end; we're not out of time.
Give us this chance, to make this right.
But now were lost in our thoughts, so I wish you well.
While they're searching for answers, I think I'm finding myself.
And the heroic valor from a conscience so free is creating a path for the ones that believe.

I'm feeling something surreal, and from the way that it sounds, the noise is echoing through this tired fading crowd.
So as this discord arises, and with ambition inside us,
please show us direction and with every intention.
This striving hope of an aspiring nation will rightfully fulfill this longing affirmation.

Anthony Cataldo

Don't Hold Back

A child is placed upon a rickety path
But he hasn't been taught to walk or talk or how to do the math
He crawls along slowly
By himself
So lonely

He never agreed to enter this world
He needs help
We all do
One child can change the world
Just give them the chance

And their light beats back the darkness
They're our future
But theirs is a treacherous path
In between the lines
Underneath the veil

In the outside of the law we shake their foundations
We can't stop at one world
We can't stop with one race
We can't leave anyone unsaved

We all have different faces
But we all run the same chase

Trae Showers

Deeper

In between truth and abstract the soul sleeps.
Only to awaken when we awaken.
The heart is our guide and everyday life is the pill that causes our great slumber.
Take us out of this life and let us run in the vast universe that is our mind.
Let us roam without a care and believe in something truly wonderful.

Where miracles are, so are the believers that see with more than just their eyes.
Whether they can see it or not, they carry the truth.
This surreal reality cannot be put into words, for words are only abstract to what is real.

Words are the tool that helps us explain, but not experience this feeling.
It is not brought about by the thick slab of uncertainty that is our senses.
It is found by something deeper.
Something too far beyond belief for the likes of us.

And right behind this, the soul sleeps waiting to be awakened so that we may come to terms with what we have been too "tired" to see.

Anthony Cataldo

"I will bring spirit into you that you may come to life."
Ez 37:5

In Search of Me

So many before me,
So where do I go to find out
They all shaped what shapes me
I would not be here without them

I want to learn from what they said.
But I don't know how to do so
I try I really do
But I only end up confused. I listen to them but do not hear their message.

I look it over but do not feel fulfilled
I go for guidance all they do is turn me away
So I will search
'Til I find out what the word actually means.

John Specker

First Step

Entering into the church is like taking our first steps into school.
We have no knowledge of what we are entering into, but we are entering in strong.
We are always hoping for the best no matter what actually turns out.
We have never seen the joy of knowledge or the terror of death.
We barely know how to spell our name.
We have not learned basic skills we need to pass through daily life.
We are like a child scared of a monster as we do not know what to expect.
Expectations can lead us into trouble as faith is all we need.
Our life can change in a matter of seconds.
As seconds go by our life is changing.
Everything about is changing except one thing: HOPE.
Our life can fall to disaster in several seconds from cruel things in this world.
As hope helps us fight desperation,
No matter how bad our situation.

Nick Ryan

"The heavens proclaim divine justice for God alone is the judge." (Ps 50:6)

Acceptance

Do we know what is important in our life?
Do we think we do?
Sports, family, friends and games
Those are all great treasures that we have

But none of those can give us true life
Like Jesus is able to with the Eucharist that he offers to us
Do we accept Jesus like few are able to do?
Or do we turn away from him, and not trust in him because it is easier that way.

Kevin Hennessy

Eucharist

The Eucharist, what's to say?
It's all been said before.
This is Jesus the son of God.
You are receiving the Lord,

when Jesus talks to us saying,
"take this bread for it is my body which has been given for you."
Then he takes a cup and says,
"take this and drink from it for it is my blood
which has been given for you."

Jesus died, he sacrificed himself for all of us.
He got rid of original sin.
He took us to the holy land.
Eucharist is close to us for it is close to him.

Brendan DuVall

Life

Life is a never ending brawl.
It will knock you off your feet.
Life can be confusing,
Life is cluster of moves.

When it comes down to it
You make the right or wrong move.
There is no way to tell which way to go
There is no way to tell where it will lead.

If you choose correctly you can prosper.
But follow that other way you will fail miserably.
You will always fail at some point in your life.
The challenge to you is how you handle it.

You can just throw a tantrum until you get what you want,
That never ends well
Or you can stand up and ask God for help
That is the best way

God will be keeping an eye on you
He will see what you don't think he sees
He will hear everything
You will have to stand up in front of him one day
And say how you handled life.

If you handle it the right way you will go right through the pearly gates.
If you don't that is up to his discretion.
He will make you wait he will make you think.
But in the end he will allow you in

Because the truth is he will always love you.
He will never turn his cheek.
He loves you, He knows that you love him.

John Specker

The Truth

There is a truth, a realization to the world
beyond this opaque cloud that is His mystery.
There are signs, hints in this world
that we surpass for our own pleasures
and unequal exaggeration for our own self worth
compared to another's.

As we share something, as simple as a meal,
we all become shared beings within the same goal.
Everything to us, is forgotten
and happiness and love become an intangible entity
that pours through the congregation as if being reborn,
alive again with a possible new outlook and drive,
an energy to live again.

Because of Him, compassion does not run dry.
It can be forgotten though,
when life becomes such a toll
upon our overworked conscience.

This is why we meet with Him and our "family",
so that we may rest, like he did.
Eat, like he did,
and go back out into that large, wondrous miracle
that is our world, reenergized to "LIVE" another day.

Anthony Cataldo

"We, indeed, are suffering because of our sins."
2Maccabees 7:32

An Ode to Hope

A boy walks down a lonely road.
No one in front of him, no one behind him.
No one to the right, and no one to the left of him.
It wasn't long ago when he was introduced to this world,
He welcomed it with childish laughter, and the innocence which so many youths seem to possess.
Little did he know what this road was . . .
He stumbles and falls; scrapes his knees.
He turns down a fork in the road, which doesn't seem to do him any better.
Now he is frightened, and skeptical of where to walk next.

The boy, now a grown man, continues down that road.
He is somewhat wiser, and has a better knowledge of what road may bring him danger, fear, sadness, and shame.
But something about those paths pull him in.
He often times lusts for those paths.
And again, he emerges from them bloody, bruised, and broken.
Now he has resorted to crawling.
He is in tears, he cries, and now shouts.
His voice echoes throughout the long, lonely road.
His memory, his mind, is now a haze of his past,
The thoughts and memories, both good and repulsive.
He now sees rays of light, breaking through the sinister clouds up ahead.
Is he dreaming?
He runs, he runs, he RUNS to it,
Believing to find treasure and happiness.

More Than A Message

But when he arrives, he falls to his knees, and begins to whimper.
What he sees, is a tree
And on that tree, is a man.
The man too, is bloody, bruised, and broken.
A crown of thorns pierces his head.
"Is this man a king?" he thought.

He looks closer at the man on the tree.
He notices nails piercing his hands and feet.
There was no doubt the light came from him.
The man on the tree was Jesus Christ on his throne, the cross.

The man looked up at Christ, and couldn't move.
Though he was nailed to this tree, and drenched in blood, it was beautiful.
The sky was blue over the cross,
And the man was in awe . . . .

Every person, man, woman, and child, are all thrown on the twisted, muddy, and rocky road of life. The life we breathe, the life we walk, *our* life. And we find Jesus in his splendid, beautiful glory.
We're all on the road, the path, the life, and the cross of Jesus Christ.

Jack Ruzicka

A New Day

Since I've been alive the whole world has felt like it is going to burst out
and cry
Everywhere there's sadness
Uncontained madness
But this one day is different
This one day is changed

I've gone inside my mind
And altered my whole mood
The whole universe looks different now
No longer held together with glue

I've blown apart false paradigms
And I'm seeing with my eyes
And I'm seeing through their lies
And I'm hearing all of your cries

False information has taken a general retreat
Life is becoming how it should be
There's still so much that we could be
But for now I'm at ease
Because today is different
And today is changed

Trae Showers

THE DRAGON

There is a boy.
He is unsure of himself.
Confusion and doubt cloud his mind, more than he even knows.
He is a bit naive, he thinks himself to be superior.
Then he encounters a problem.
He faces it thinking that he can take on the world if he had to.
He fails miserably.
Writhing in self pity, the boy continues to fight.
Then he realizes that he is alone.
Feeling shunned and defeated, the boy leaves.
As he walks away, he attempts to think of why his foe fled.
As he recalls his battle, he remembers he was with friends.
He remembers that he has no enemies.
With friends like his, he didn't need enemies.
The boy leaves.
He meets a woman, her name is Mary.
She invites him to join her community.
The boy accepts.
It is not long before the boy emerges.
The boy is now a Dragon.
He knows that he can take on his problems now.
He has new friends.
Mary has shown him who he really is.

James Muehlenkamp

Baptism

Baptism is the first step in a long life journey.
Your parents make the choice for you to start it.
You learn slowly what it means as you grow.
Some may never truly know. You agree to follow Christ's message
knowing that you may be put through many messes.

It is one of the biggest choices you will ever make.
And it comes before we can even think.
You vow to God and he will save your soul. Your godparents say the
baptismal vows in hope he will guide you.

John Specker

Act

Shout out but don't raise your voice
Jump and dance and shake the dirt floor
Send emotions through the sky and activate thirty more
Govern your thoughts and forge a new mindset
Shot paradigms broken by the score

Peril and ignorance lie around the bend
But there is a different path to take
Different choices to make
There are no civilians
It's the war of humanity
We're fighting for our sanity

Open your eyes to the scorched battlefield
Find your rickety bridge
Check over the ridge
The depths below beckon
Darkness lies at the bottom of the sea
We've been swimming for thousands of years
We're running out of breath

Trae Showers

Act IV-Strength

"By educating the mind and the heart, the school can form men who in turn work at changing the very structures of their society to ensure a community of justice and reconciliation."

Blessed William Joseph Chaminade

"All this you were allowed to see that you might know the Lord is God and there is no other."
Deuteronomy 4:35

Southside Dragons

I GIVE TO YOU

I am the Lord. The only Lord I stand alone. If you are the Lord I give you my heart. You alone can have my mind. You alone may have my soul. And I give you my strength. I give it all to you My Lord.

Brendan DuVall

A Reclamation of Our Demise

I do not stand on a platform, a pedestal.

I stand on the soil, given to us by our Father. This is the time, the place, the everlasting battleground.

We fight not for ourselves, but for every last person on this desolate and forsaken planet.

We fight not because we know the evil of the enemy, but because we do not know the enemy at all.

We shall sacrifice ourselves to the fight, the passion, and the dream.

They have the numbers, but we have the heart. They have the arms, but we have our minds, our souls. They own this land, but we own its meaning, the purpose.

We band together as brothers and sisters and not fight, but surrender to the timeless battle against ourselves.

Anthony Cataldo

Flare up Great Flame

Flare up great flame
Consume my soul
Take me from this deep dark hole
Take away these chains
Free me from my bones
Show me the light
Which is seen
Only by those
Who open their eyes
All others not awake
Continue to live in a fake
World driven by desire
It is not our right to leave them behind
For this Spirit, this Lord, this Christ who has been so kind
Calls us to
Reach for those souls
Trapped across a great divide
And save them not from their sins

But from a world
Which has lied to them
Giving what they do not need
But taking what is always needed
So flare up great flame
Consume their souls
Take them from that deep dark hole.

Conor Cashner

"You who dwell in the shelter of the Most High . . .
Say to the Lord, 'My refuge and fortress, my God in whom I trust'."
Psalm 91:1-2

Beside You

The Father, the Son, the Holy Spirit
Say it out loud so the whole world may hear it
Don't keep it inside you
Share it with everyone
Help them stand beside you

Be a leader of a new group
One that follows God
One that listens to his word
One that accepts all people willing to join
Allow them to stand beside you

Take your solid troop
And make an even bigger group
So that God will never be forgotten
So that you can live life of hope
And everyone will want to stand beside you

Kevin Hennessy

Forgiveness

Being stuck is the worst feeling
Can't go around it
You can't look the other way
You know you're caught
You are unable to accept
You try to move side to side
You try to jump
When that fails you try to dive
When it comes time
You need to face it
Accept it
For those who don't
They will always be in that worthless battle
Knowing they will never win
Eventually they will give up
But they have lost so much more
If they had accepted it
They would have been happier
But not now they are lonely
The people they started the fight with
Left and accepted it long ago
They finally accepted it
But now they have a new battle to fight
To get the ones they lost back
They start this one like the last one
But will it be different this time
They are gaining ground
They are growing happier and happier
They are starting to move faster
There is still that voice though

That one you try to ignore
The little thing that holds you back
Makes you make the wrong move
If you listen to it you fail
That's what happens
Once again they are stuck
No way out
Just
Plain
STUCK

John Specker

The Greatest Defeats

The greatest defeats take mere seconds,
They are the failed ordeals,
The opportunities missed.

You look back again and again,
Wondering what you could have done,
Where did you fail, or did you fail at all?

Would that last exertion,
One last show of strength, will, force,
Make the difference?
One will never know.

Conor Cashner